The Three
Rivers of Zambia

Rob Waring, *Series Ed*

T0052345

NATIONAL
GEOGRAPHIC
LEARNING

Australia · Brazil · Canada · Mexico · Singapore · United Kingdom · United States

Words to Know

This story is set in the country of Zambia, Africa. It's about three major rivers there: the Luangwa [luaŋwa], the Kafue [kafueɪ], and the Zambezi [zæmbɪzi].

A **Animals of Zambia.** Here are some wild animals you will find in the story. Label the picture with the words in the box.

an antelope	elephants	a hippopotamus
a crocodile	gazelles	lions

2. _____

1. _____

3. _____

B **Along the River.** Read the paragraph. Then complete the sentences with the correct form of the underlined words.

The banks that lie along the rivers of Zambia are full of wildlife. These river areas are natural habitats for several animals. Many species of wild animals and birds live on or near them. Because of this, they're also an excellent place for predators to find a meal. Over the years, the Zambian government has made much of this land into national parks and animal reserves. It's the best way to keep the animals safe from hunters.

1. A _____ is an animal that hunts, kills, and eats other animals.

2. The _____ of a river are the land areas along the edges of the water.

3. An _____ is a place where animals can live freely while being protected.

4. The area in which an animal or plant normally lives is its _____.

5. A _____ is a specific group of living things that have similar characteristics.

6. The animals and plants living independently of people in a natural setting are called _____.

4. _____

5. _____

6. _____

The beautiful country of Zambia lies in the center of southern Africa. It doesn't have a coast; it's nowhere near an ocean, and has land all around it. Despite this, Zambia is a country that is largely shaped by water. How can this be? The country of Zambia is heavily influenced by three major rivers: the Luangwa, the Kafue, and the Zambezi. It's these three great rivers that give Zambia its special character. This is the story of these three rivers and the people and the wildlife that live along them.

🎧 CD 2, Track 01

The Luangwa River flows to the south from the northeastern end of Zambia. The waters of the Luangwa are full of wildlife. One can find hippopotamuses, or 'hippos', cooling themselves in the river's water and lions relaxing on its banks. Groups of gazelles walk carefully into the dirty waters of the river. However, they'd better be careful; there's one more kind of animal nearby—the crocodile!

Crocodiles are extremely dangerous; they can easily jump up and kill a gazelle that is standing at the edge of the water. In fact, the Luangwa River makes an excellent hunting ground for predators of all types. Why? Both large and small animals depend on the river to survive. All of these species have one thing in common: they must gather along the river's banks to get the water that they need to live.

The wildlife along the banks of the Luangwa is wonderful and varied. It's common to see elephants walking in the river and beautiful, large birds. Unfortunately, as people move into areas that used to be wild, these wild animal populations are beginning to be threatened. Human beings are moving into the animals' habitat, and that means that the animals must often move out.

Fortunately, the government of Zambia is protecting important animal habitats along the Luangwa River. Large portions of the Luangwa have been made into national parks and animal reserves. In these parks and reserves, animals have enough space to move around freely and live healthily and happily. More importantly, people cannot hunt them in these protected areas. This means that the animals of the Luangwa are safe—at least for now.

Infer Meaning

1. What does the writer mean by 'these animal populations are beginning to be threatened'?

2. What does the writer mean by 'the animals are safe—at least for now'?

While the Luangwa lies in the eastern part of Zambia, the next major river can be found directly in the middle of the country. The Kafue River is in the center of Zambia. Around it, huge, level areas of land known as the Kafue Flats have been protected as national parks and animal reserves. Here, seasonal **floods**[1] support the environment of many animals, including beautiful and rare types of antelope. One can also find hundreds of species of birds. Because of this, the government of Zambia takes very good care of these native species' habitats.

The waters of the Kafue do more than just support the local wildlife, however. The Kafue also produces **hydroelectricity**[2] for the country. In addition, the river's water supports **irrigation**[3] systems for farms in the area. In this way, the water of the Kafue is essential for the people of the region: it helps to provide the electricity they need and the food that they eat.

---

[1] **flood:** when water covers an area that is usually dry; especially when a river becomes too full
[2] **hydroelectricity:** power made from the energy of moving water
[3] **irrigation:** the providing of water for an area of land so that food can be grown

The Luangwa and the Kafue are both great rivers, but they both eventually join an even greater river: the Zambezi. The Zambezi is Africa's fourth largest **river basin**[4] and it starts as a small and slow river in the north of Zambia. As it moves toward Zambia's southern edge, its water flows gently. In this area, the Zambezi serves as a kind of 'water road' for nearby communities who use it for everyday purposes. People use small boats to carry things between villages and to travel up and down the river.

---

[4]**river basin:** a long, natural area of land in which a river flows

The Zambezi may start slowly, but a few hundred miles down the river, this gentle body of water becomes extremely fast and powerful. At this point, the changing river becomes one of the world's great **waterfalls**.[5] From a distance, the falling water looks like smoke, and makes a lot of noise. This is probably why the local people call the waterfall the 'smoke that **thunders**'[6] in their native language. The rest of the world knows this **spectacular**[7] waterfall as Victoria Falls.

---

[5]**waterfall:** a point where water drops from a higher to lower area
[6]**thunder:** make a continuous loud noise
[7]**spectacular:** impressive and beautiful; fantastic

ANGOLA

ZAMBEZI R.

KAFUE R.

Z A M

KAFUE FLATS

VICTORIA FALLS

TANZANIA

NORTH
LUANGWA
NATIONAL
PARK

SOUTH
LUANGWA
NATIONAL
PARK

LUANGWA R.

B I A

MALAWI

ZIMBABWE

MOZAMBIQUE

15

In 1855, British explorer Dr. David Livingstone became the first known European to see the impressive Victoria Falls. He named the waterfall after the queen of England at the time, Queen Victoria. The nearby town of Livingstone was named after Dr. Livingstone. Since that time, the town has become a main starting point for tourists who want to explore the river. Some visitors go there to walk around the beautiful green areas near the falls. Others want to see Victoria Falls up close from a train that passes by the top of the falls. Some of the more daring tourists even come to **kayak**[8] on the great Zambezi River.

Victoria Falls is one of the largest waterfalls in the world and is truly spectacular to see. The volume of water that flows through this amazing natural wonder is spectacular as well. Approximately **one million gallons**[9] of water fall over the **355-foot**[10]-high falls every second!

---

[8]**kayak:** travel in a light, narrow boat, usually made for one person
[9]**one million gallons:** 3,785,411.8 liters (1 gallon = 3.78 liters)
[10]**355 feet:** 110.1 meters (1 foot = 0.31 meters)

Fact Check: True or false?

1. Livingstone was the first man to ever see the waterfall.

2. The waterfall was named after David Livingstone.

3. The waterfall is one of the largest in the world.

4. It is a popular tourist attraction.

It's easy to understand why people want to visit the huge, crashing waters of Victoria Falls. However, the Zambezi doesn't just stop at the famous waterfall. From Victoria Falls, it continues its long journey to the Indian Ocean. It flows through several other countries before it reaches the coast. Along the way, it is joined by the two other great rivers of Zambia: the Kafue and then the Luangwa. Individually, each of these rivers is important in any number of ways. Together, these three rivers help to make Zambia what it is today.

After You Read

1. On page 4, the word 'character' can be replaced by:
   A. person
   B. threat
   C. wisdom
   D. style

2. What is the purpose of the description on page 4?
   A. to talk about rivers
   B. to introduce the story
   C. to teach about wildlife
   D. to show the Zambia coast

3. Animals do each of the following in the Luangwa River EXCEPT:
   A. sleep
   B. kill
   C. stand
   D. cool down

4. When humans move _____, animals must often move _____.
   A. on, up
   B. to, also
   C. off, in
   D. in, out

5. How do national parks and reserves protect animals?
   A. People can't hunt in them.
   B. Animals can't kill each other in them.
   C. Food is provided for the animals in them.
   D. New animals are introduced to the wild in them.

6. Which is NOT a good heading for paragraph 2 on page 11?
   A. Floods Good for Animals
   B. River Provides for Farms
   C. Rare Animals on the Kafue
   D. Many Depend on Kafue

7. On page 12, 'they' refers to:
   A. the Zambezi and the Kafue
   B. the Luangwa, the Kafue, and the Zambezi
   C. the Luangwa and the Zambezi
   D. the Kafue and the Luangwa

8. Some Zambian people travel _____ the Zambezi daily.
   A. on
   B. in
   C. of
   D. from

9. What does Victoria Falls look like?
   A. a kayak
   B. smoke
   C. thunder
   D. the Luangwa

10. Why does the writer give details about the amount of water in Victoria Falls?
    A. to explain that kayaking is fun
    B. to show how powerful the waterfall is
    C. to introduce the subject of Dr. Livingstone
    D. to give an example of a typical waterfall

11. On page 19, the word 'Individually' can be replaced by:
    A. Alone
    B. Together
    C. Closely
    D. Apart

12. Why does the writer think these three rivers are so important?
    A. They go to the Indian Ocean.
    B. They each have a waterfall.
    C. They make Zambia special.
    D. all of the above

TAKE A WALKING TOUR WITH 'TOUR ZAMBIA'!

Most tourists who visit Zambia come to see the amazing wildlife. Unfortunately, most of these visitors are driven everywhere and can only get close to nature when they stop. With Tour Zambia's walking tours, you'll get a chance to examine the local habitat of many different species up close! Each walking tour is led by a two-person team: an expert in local wildlife, and a guard who keeps everyone safe. With our walking tours, you'll have the opportunity to explore Zambia's national parks and animal reserves in a safe, satisfying environment.

Fast Facts about Zambia	
Full Name	Republic of Zambia
Area	752,614 square kilometers (290,586 square miles)
Population (2005 estimate)	11,227,000
Capital City	Lusaka
Official Language	English
Money	Zambian Kwacha

NATURE PARK TOUR

Our walking tour of the South Luangwa National Park begins very early. We start the day at 5:00 A.M. with a healthy outdoor breakfast. From there, we take a walk in the eastern section of the park. There are few roads in this area, so there's less chance of seeing other tourists. What you will see are animals: antelope, lions, and even hippopotamuses! After a relaxing lunch, we continue our explorations in the western section of the park. The day ends back at the park entrance, where we'll drive you safely back to your hotel for a good night's rest.

RIVER TOUR

On the Tour Zambia's River Walk tour, we fly you from Lusaka to the Mwaleshi Airport. From there, it's a four-hour walk to Mwaleshi Camp. Once we arrive, guests can rest or go for a swim in the Mwaleshi River.

The next morning, we go on a five-mile walk down the river to see some of its amazing wildlife. Visitors can often see one of Africa's most famous predators—the lion! Lunch is cooked over an open fire and served on the banks of the Mwaleshi. After lunch, guests have a choice of either walking back to camp, or riding back with one of the guides. The next day, everyone flies back to Lusaka to get ready for their next adventure.

WHY WAIT?

Don't miss your chance to see the most exciting wildlife reserves in Africa. Zambia is waiting for you!

CD 2, Track 02

Word Count: 338
Time: _____

Vocabulary List

antelope (2, 11)
banks (3, 7, 8)
crocodile (2, 7)
elephant (2, 8)
flood (11)
gazelle (2, 7)
habitat (3, 8, 11)
hippopotamus (2, 7)
hydroelectricity (11)
irrigation (11)
kayak (16)
lion (2, 7)
predator (3, 7)
reserve (3, 8, 11)
river basin (12)
species (3, 7, 11)
spectacular (14, 16)
thunder (14)
waterfall (14, 16, 17, 19)
wildlife (3, 4, 7, 8, 11)